# DEFY FEAR

## Spirit of Entrepreneurship

Cuffee the Magnificent

L.J. Simpson

**CUFFEE MEDIA GROUP**

# DEDICATED TO

All the risk takers and trendsetters that have come before us

# CONTENTS

# A GOOD DAY

Today was the oddest day. For the first time in years, I was the only one working my electronics store, Tech-Nine. My store manager and partner in day-to-day operations, Whitney, is out recuperating from foot surgery. Whitney will be back before the summer's end, but our part-timer Alex is leaving for State U in the fall. We are already understaffed and when Alex leaves we will definitely need to hire. But, who has the time to interview candidates? There are a thousand other things on my plate. Anyway, where was I?

I saw a boy no more than fourteen years old with the poise of a pink panther. He was attempting to shoplift, but he was doing a terrible job at it. To be honest, I would have been very angry if I wasn't so tired. I slipped from behind the counter and headed towards the front of the store in order to flank him.

Approaching him with little desire for stealth, I just blurted out, "What do you think you're doing?"

He turned with a shocked look in his eyes.

"What do you think you're doing?" I repeated.

"Do what?"

"What?...You slipped that ten-inch tablet in your knapsack. All is forgiven if you just return the items. However, you may never return, agreed?"

He stood there looking like he was thinking something a thousand times over. And then he looked up at me and said, "Give me a job."

"What job?"

"Give me a job."

"You just tried to steal from me, and now you want me to offer you a job?"

"If I had a job, I could pay for it."

And I stopped. He felt he needed this object so much he had to steal it, but was willing to work for it? Now I was thinking this a thousand times over. He wasn't even sure of the nature of work we did, but only wanted a "job" so he could buy a tablet.

"What do you plan to do with the tablet?" I asked.

"Sell it."

"So you don't even need the tablet at all, and if you had the job, you wouldn't buy the tablet, correct?"

"Maybe...but I definitely wouldn't sell it if I bought it."

It was sound logic. This kid had some nerve and to top it off asking to work alongside me? Over my ten years in business, I know that a determined and risk adverse mentality is invaluable. So I thought to myself, "why not hire the kid?"

Well, we didn't hire Martin right away because of his attempted theft. We met his parents whose response was as shocked as mine though we reached an agreement. Martin's parents let him work in the shop for 15 hours a week until he worked off the cost of the tablet. From then on he would receive a regular paycheck.

Martin took to his position with such enthusiasm and excitement that it rekindled my passion for entrepreneurship. Whitney even had a quicker recovery, being eager to work again and meet Martin. Although Martin only worked with us for two years, in that time he turned around his academic performance graduating with honors. Martin followed Alex to college with a scholarship to State U, double majoring in political science and business. Every summer, he would come back home and work in the store as a full-time clerk and part-time consultant. It allowed him to apply what he was learning in school in the real world and also help the business improve.

Hiring Martin didn't seem logical at first but it turned out to be a great decision. It reminded me why I went into business for myself in the first place. My business is small, but we're proud of the work we're doing and the...

REHH REHH!!!!
REHH REHH!!!!
REHH REHH!!!!
REHH REHH!!!!

I switch off the alarm as XM radio cycles through comedy podcasts. Sitting upright and stretching, I look at the time knowing it's six in the morning. It was only a dream, but it felt so real. I can still see Whitney, Alex, and Martin's smiling faces. The smell of duct tape and staples from newly delivered inventory was so vivid. I can feel the joy of making a difference in my community while being a successful entrepreneur.

I stand up from my bed and glance at the small business loan brochure on my nightstand. Usually, I always feel a deep sense of anxiety and dread when thinking about starting my business. But after this dream, I feel like this can really happen. I think I can really do this.

It's going to be a good day.

\*       \*       \*

The story above was merely a fictional account representing the experience of many entrepreneurs. Although it was only a dream, the narrator experienced how a business can apply the Economics of Happiness and operate with a deeper purpose than just making money. Awaking from her dream, she felt a new sense of hope and optimism as the fear began to fall away.

This booklet outlines and provides steady instruction in order to utilize business as a tool to defy fear and realize your dreams. Turning the page is only the first step in defying your fear. You must dream a dream and never let it go.

# STEP 1

## DREAM A DREAM AND NEVER LET IT GO

Dream BIG! Some of you may already roll your eyes when you hear the call to "dream big." But that feeling is only doubt slipping in. Address your fear first so that you may dare to dream big. Want to end world hunger? Open your own gift shop? How about creating a line of luxury accessories? Whatever your dream, goal or vision be, don't let your doubts stifle your ability to acknowledge what you truly desire.

In order to create something from nothing it is important you choose a venture that will require all your focus. Choosing a smaller goal may seem less overwhelming but you must step outside of what you know you can do and attempt what you literally think you can do. If you've found your vision, apply this test.   If someone you loved deeply was trapped in a burning building, you wouldn't think twice about how you could save them.   You wouldn't be concerned about your personal safety or the potential for injury. You would risk your life to save them.   So the question we pose to you is, would you be willing to save your dream in the same way?

Have you found your dream and vision yet?   If the answer is NO, don't stress about it, just keep exploring until you find it.   Many times you won't find your dream by exploring the what, but the rather the why.  Have a definitive answer to the question of "Why do I want to own a business"?  The answer to that question can reveal what truly motivates you. If money is your answer you must dream bigger, because money will not buy you complete happiness.

# STEP 2

## MONEY WILL NOT BUY YOU COMPLETE HAPPINESS

Have you ever relocated for a position because the pay was better, but in the end you weren't happy with the town you moved to? Were you willing to commute the "hour drive" realizing it's actually a distance of ninety miles? Ever take on a position for the pay even though its responsibilities overtook the management of your personal life?

These and similar situations may sound all too familiar. They may not seem so bad at the surface but over time can wear on you physiologically, psychologically and spiritually. Stress can be carried over into your personal life and your family could find themselves subjected to it. Your physical health could be affected negatively, as well as, a decline in your demeanor and social interactions.

What are your main concerns about the dream you have envisioned? Is it a lack of finances? Financial stability for your family? Student loans? You should not worry about what people will think. Don't think about if it's possible or how hard it will be. These are only distractions. Cast these fears aside and sail on to destiny. Don't let anything stop you and know that anything can be accomplished with time and patience. Do not simply wait around for your opportunity, chip away at your dream so that you will be prepared when the time is right. If you can't afford to open a store location, start an online store. If you are lacking financial or marketing skills, find a consultant. If you need more experience, then volunteer working for a business similar to the one you will start. Rome wasn't built in a day and neither will your business.

Chip away at the big dream a piece at a time, but get started today. Get excited about creating the future you want and keep an eye on the finish line. "Entrepreneurship is about taking what excites you in life and turning it into capital"- Sir Richard Branson. Becoming a multi-millionaire is not and should not be the goal. If a loaf of bread cost a million dollars due to hyperinflation, then being a millionaire would be pointless.

Our true desire is not to collect coins or change the number on bank statements. What a boring and dull existence! What we really want is a millionaire lifestyle and quality of life. Again, money is neither the aim nor endgame, it is the byproduct of using business as a tool.

# STEP 3

## USE BUSINESS AS A TOOL

Let's consider Richard Branson, the founder of Virgin Group, who started his empire in a church basement. Today, Branson is the chairman of a company that offers entrepreneurs, the opportunity to bring their ideas to life in the areas of music, science and art. "Chance favors the prepared mind, the more you practice the better you become."- Sir Richard Branson.  This may again draw a negative response if you believe Branson's success is far too large for the common man. However, Branson's mission in life is to create platforms for artists & entrepreneurs that most investors would reject.

Without even considering money, for what reason do you want to be an entrepreneur? Do you know why? Chances are that your answer may be closely tied to something called, social capital. Why should you be familiar with the term social capital? If you click through the link, a TED Talk featuring Dr. Meg Jay expounds upon this subject in greater detail. For the moment, think of social capital as your overall quality of life.

Capital, we'll first define as a form of asset. Assets are resources used to generate income or provide a future benefit. To be social is to engage and interact with other people. Thus, social capital refers to the quality of connections you build professionally and personally. What if you're naturally introverted? Even introverts find a way to define themselves within their community and establish a network of colleagues, peers and friends. Social capital has nothing to do with being outgoing and bubbly. It is about providing significant value to the lives of people around you.

So we must make yet another paradigm shift. We must consider entrepreneurship as a social institution and marry the ideas of Abraham Maslow and Adam Smith.

Before you climb the hierarchy of needs, first get out of your comfort zone.

# STEP 4

## GET OUT OF YOUR COMFORT ZONE

When you think and act outside of your normal boundaries, fear will arise. Usually those boundaries are made of fear. But the further and more frequently you move outside your comfort zone, the more your confidence will grow. In order to expand your perimeter, you must open your mind to new ways of thinking. More information doesn't hurt anyone, it only provides options. Even after you've read this entire booklet you could choose not to change your life, but at least that choice is now yours. Taking the time to read this booklet shows that you desire to defy your fear. You always test the waters before you swim into the deep. Coming out of your comfort zone takes time because we are creatures of habit and repetition is crucial in the learning process. Work diligently at your business idea spending time to understand the market, scout locations, study competitor models, join your local chamber, volunteer in the industry, etc.

This could take months or years due to full-time employment, children, debt, and mortgage. Some of you may face these concerns in combination and they all require your time and money. Remember to enjoy your family and take care of all your responsibilities, but in the meantime you will chip away at the big goal. By the time you're able to launch your venture, you will have grown your social capital. Learning your market, gaining knowledge through volunteering and securing a great location all can help you get started. You may actually be able to begin making the shift gradually into managing your own enterprise. Whether you do so part-time or leap confidently into your business, do so with passion.

We must now turn our eyes to understanding the value of qualitative versus quantitative. Qualitative stems from quality and is graded by completeness. Quantitative stems from quantity which we will identify as a specific amount. If I were to ask you how much money would it take to be completely whole and happy for the rest of your life could you give a dollar amount? We dare any and all number crunchers and bean counters to provide a number. Even if you were to calculate an amount, is that all you think your life is worth? Now, if I were to ask you what it would take for you to be completely whole and happy for the rest of your life, what would your answer be? I'll take a shot in the dark and say you probably thought of your loved ones, family, friends, or maybe an idea or creation you wanted to share with the world.

The late Ray Anderson, the Founder & CEO of Interface Inc., is an example of a business leader that dared to go beyond his comfort zone. He is known for turning Dalton, Georgia into the "Carpet Capital of the World." When we look at carpets we mainly detect the fiber, pattern, texture and color, as all of these factors influence our decisions. Anderson looked at carpet in even greater depth, questioning it's vinyl backing, carbon footprint during manufacturing and distribution processes. After reading The Ecology of Commerce, written by Paul Hawken, Anderson underwent a paradigm shift about his company's operational methods. He decided to hire a team of environmentalists to perform an assessment on their overall waste. Upon receiving results, he then hired the group to oversee the project and achieve the directive of sustainability. Click the link for a TED Talk on Anderson's discussion on his going green initiative. Even at sixty years old, Anderson was willing to open his mind to new ways of thinking and with the position of power he held courageously made an effort to become eco-friendly.

It can become overwhelming to think of the daunting task at hand but that's why it is important to find a routine and stick to the process.

# STEP 5

## FIND A ROUTINE AND STICK TO THE PROCESS

Think back to a task you thought you would never complete. Was it an undergraduate degree? Masters? An enlistment contract? Raising a family?

Just think back on a time when you felt as though you were incapable of a task, yet rose to the occasion by keeping your eye on the prize. We are creatures of habit and in order to break old habits we have to learn new, more challenging habits. If you're burnt out of working in an industry where you don't have the opportunity to exercise your exceptional leadership skills, creativity, business savvy, craftsmanship, it is important to read on carefully.

In order to take the next step you must find a new routine. This again speaks to the "chip away" mentality we spoke of before. This may require creating a schedule so that you may set aside time for yourself everyday or at least three to four times a week to become acclimated to what will eventually become your daily routine full-time.

A famous quote from Les Brown states, "The richest and greatest place on earth is the graveyard. It's full of people who never acted on their dreams because they were too shy and too comfortable. Their dreams are buried with them." When your venture is in its early stages you will suffer setbacks and oversights for things you just didn't take into account. For instance, employees could abandon ship, legal claims/disputes could arise and/or equipment could break or require repair.

You must not let these day-to-day nuances discourage you or keep you down.

You must learn from your mistakes.

# STEP 6

## LEARN FROM YOUR MISTAKES

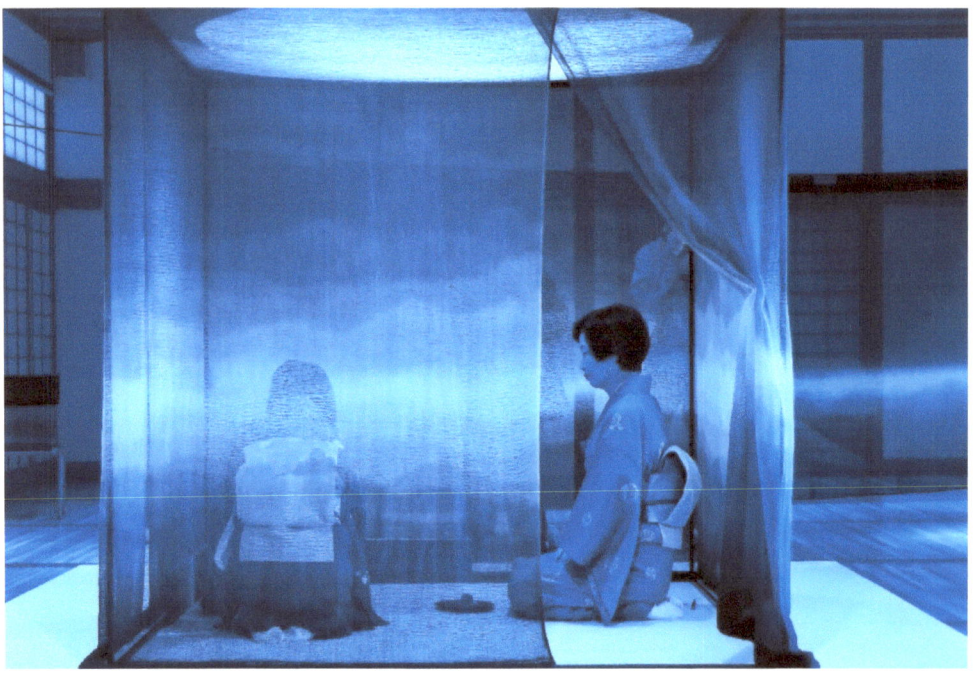

At this stage you have fully embraced fear as an ever present aspect of your life. You will never be rid of fear, but the idea is to understand why it exists and go from there. If you come to a juncture prompted by fear you must decide whether or not your concerns are legitimate; Step 2. Reaching an understanding of this concept is the most important step in defeating fear. You will have suffered setbacks as well as your share of "Ah-Ha!" moments and entrepreneurship is no longer a mystery to you. With an understanding of how to use business as a tool, your mind has the power to turn setbacks into hard earned wisdom.

Some of the worst ideas come from the best of intentions, so avoid making unnecessary changes. Any and all outside advice offered may not be the best course of action. This is not said in order to define the rules of "staying true" rather as a warning against making bold decisions when you have not thought the matters through. It may be necessary to create small changes that lead you out of your plateau and refresh your business venture. Maybe that change is working on your customer service skills or perhaps you've outgrown your location. Whatever the small changes may be, do so with care to avoid harming your business.

Equally as important is measuring your qualitative growth. Take a look to see where you started and see how far you've come. If you're business idea has been a success then that is great news and most certainly the result of diligence and hard work. However, we also want to keep in mind the concept of qualitative versus quantitative, meaning we want to view things more holistically.

Has your business venture brought back the spark of life? Has it affected your personal life in a positive way? Remember, you should be passionate about your idea because the qualitative gains you earn while working towards your dream will be immeasurable. Learning from your mistakes is as important to growth as learning from your successes. When you harp over the small things in life, it takes your focus off of the big picture and stifles your capacity for creativity. Keep things in perspective; find the lesson to avoid repeating your mistakes and

Continue To Grow.

# STEP 7

## CONTINUE TO GROW

When we mention the word growth our minds think of something increasing in size or amount, as mentioned in Step 4. This mindset goes against conventional wisdom but we must remember growth is not always defined numerically.

The entrepreneur in our introduction was living a dream within a dream. She had big dreams and began chipping away at them by simply looking into business loans. Remember qualitative versus quantitative and consider the growth of your sphere of influence during this time. If you find yourself hitting a plateau, remember that you have limitless potential and it may be time to take an assessment of your dream . If things are stagnant it could be time to face fear again.

Your aim is not to reinvent the wheel but rather find your x-factor or the latent gift you possess, your passion, and use business as a tool to generate social capital. The qualitative benefits of your life are immeasurable and should be taken into account during your period of plateau. Living fearless is the best way to live. Continue being a student of your passion, because this is the road to mastery. Remember, you have limitless potential!

It is important that you repeat each step in the cycle on a regular basis. Over time temporary situations and circumstances can/will cause you to lose sight of your dream.

When you feel fear and doubt creeping in again, start again at Step 1.

Defy fear at any cost.

## ABOUT CUFFEE MEDIA GROUP

Cuffee Media Group is a marketing and innovation company founded by Cuffee the Magnificent. Cuffee, and his team, work with entrepreneurs that share his mission to create a more innovative and creative society. The company's services include marketing campaigns, sales management, and business education. The majority of the company's clients are media, entertainment, education, or technology companies.

www.CuffeeMediaGroup.com

www.CuffeeMagnificent.com

www.ingramcontent.com/pod-product-compliance
Lightning Source LLC
Chambersburg PA
CBHW050424180526
45159CB00005B/2405